ARTIST TRANSCRIPTIONS

PIANO · BASS · DRUMS

Bill Evans THE

Trio

1959-1961

C000104215

Music transcriptions by Liam Noble, Chris Baron, and Artemis Music Ltd.

Cover Photo: Mike Byergo

ISBN-13: 978-0-634-05179-1
ISBN-10: 0-634-05179-2

HAL·LEONARD®
CORPORATION

7777 W. BLUEMOUND RD. P.O. BOX 13819 MILWAUKEE, WI 53213

Visit Hal Leonard Online at
www.halleonard.com

DISCOGRAPHY

SONG TITLE	RECORDING
Alice In Wonderland	*Sunday At The Village Vanguard/* Riverside (June 25, 1961)
Autumn Leaves (Les Feuilles Mortes)	*Portrait In Jazz/* Riverside (December 28, 1959)
How Deep Is The Ocean (How High Is The Sky)	*Explorations/* Riverside (February 2, 1961)
Nardis	*Explorations/* Riverside (February 2, 1961)
Peri's Scope	*Portrait In Jazz/* Riverside (December 28, 1959)
Solar	*Sunday At The Village Vanguard/* Riverside (June 25, 1961)
Waltz For Debby	*Waltz For Debby/* Riverside (June 25, 1961)
When I Fall In Love	*Portrait In Jazz/* Riverside (December 28, 1959)

THE Bill Evans Trio
1959-1961

CONTENTS

Alice In Wonderland
from Walt Disney's ALICE IN WONDERLAND

Words by Bob Hilliard
Music by Sammy Fain

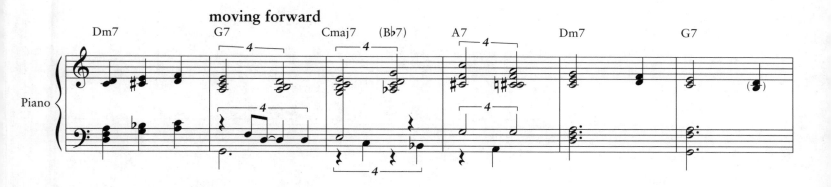

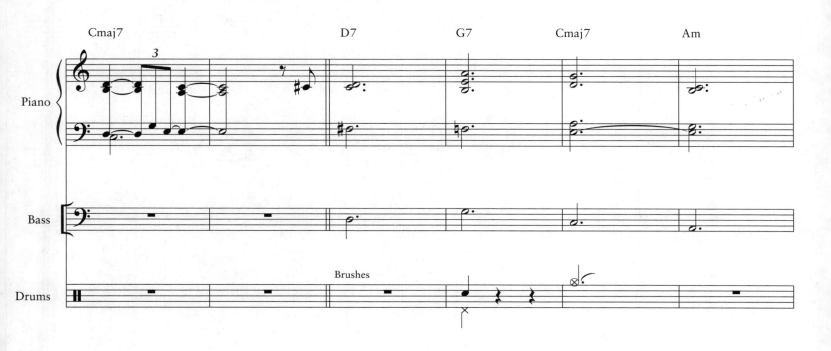

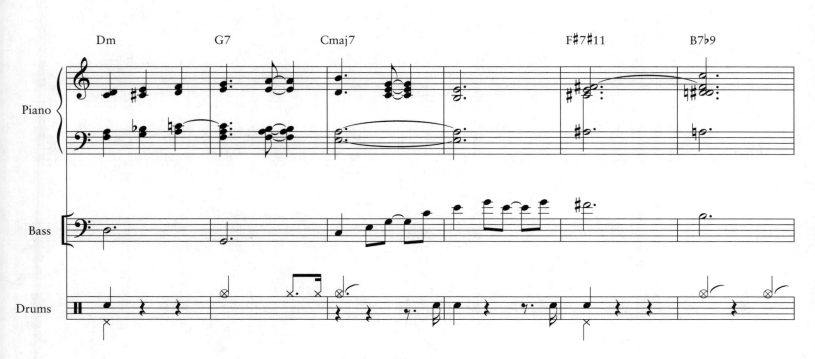

6

9

10

11

14

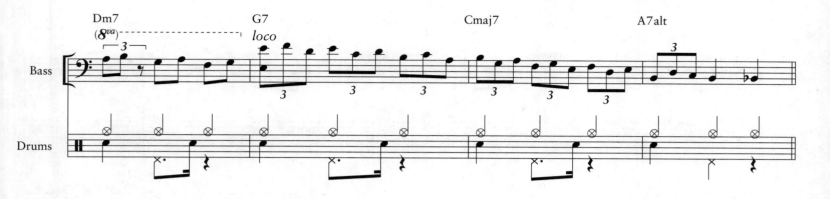

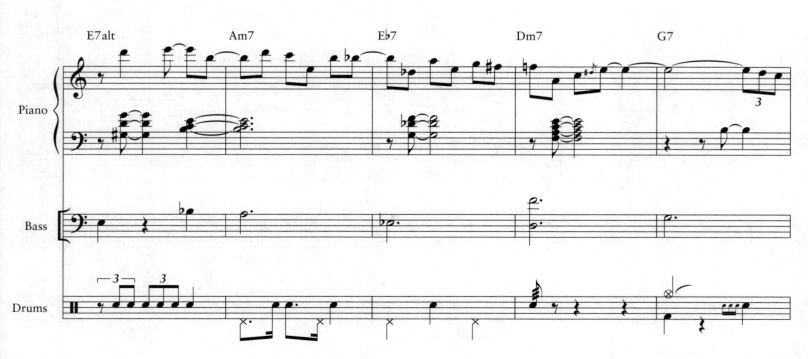

23

30

Autumn Leaves (Les Feuilles Mortes)

English lyric by Johnny Mercer
French lyric by Jacques Prevert
Music by Joseph Kosma

44

49

How Deep Is The Ocean
(How High Is The Sky)

Words and Music by Irving Berlin

Nardis

By Miles Davis

74

82

Peri's Scope

Music by Bill Evans

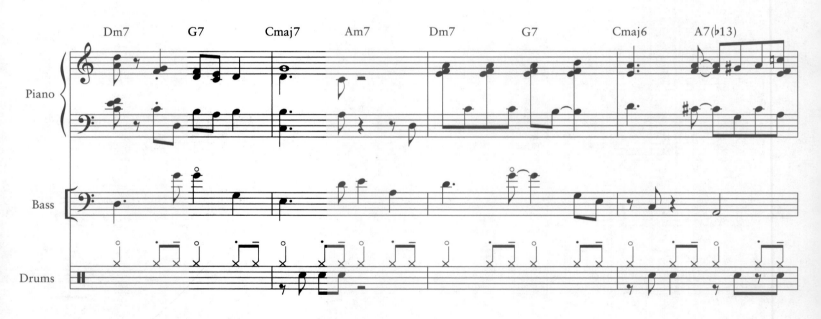

Solar

By Miles Davis

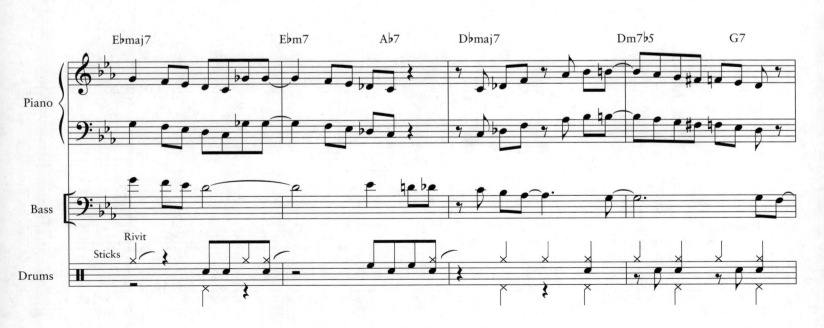

100

107

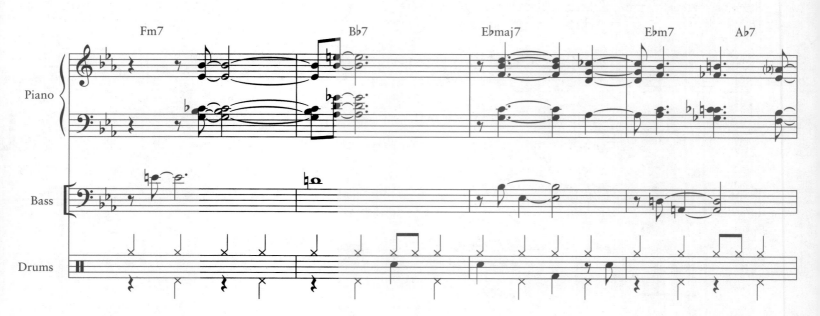

130

Waltz For Debby

Lyric by Gene Lees
Music by Bill Evans

140

146

150

151

154

155

156

159

When I Fall In Love

Words by Edward Heyman
Music by Victor Young

* All approximate – played rubato

164

166